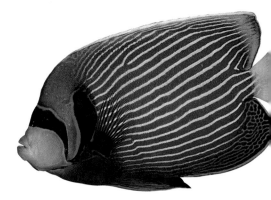

AMAZING ANIMALS

COLORS

WRITTEN BY

REBECCA L. GRAMBO

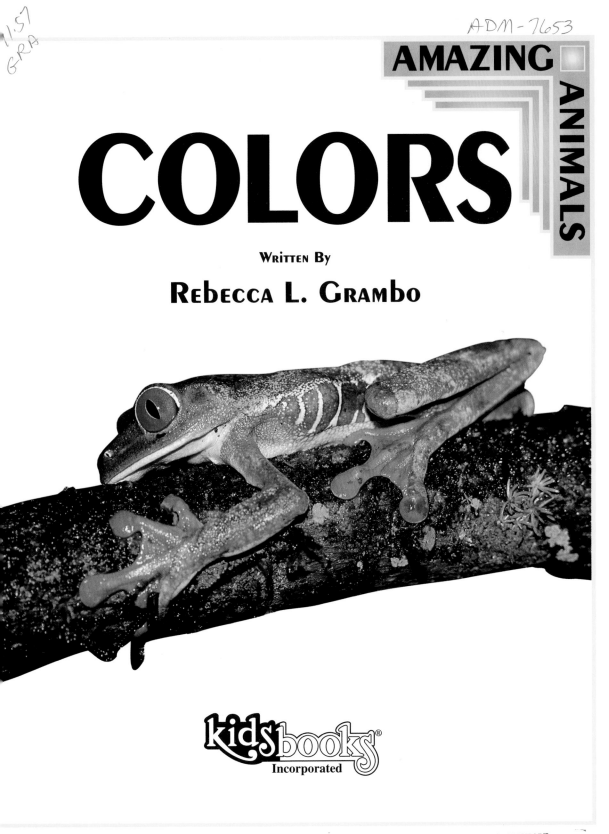

kidsbooks®
Incorporated

People come in different colors. Our hair, eyes, and skin can all be different from those of our friends. But animals come in many more colors and patterns than people.

This tree frog has lots of colors. It even has red eyes and orange toes! But when the tree frog rests, it sits with its eyes closed. Then the bright colors are hidden, and the green frog blends in with the tree in which it sits.

If something startles the frog, it open its eyes and moves. This sudden flash of bright colors can scare a predator, and give the frog time to escape.

Some animals show very little color. You can almost see right through the ghost catfish below. It is transparent (trans-PAIR-ent). Transparent animals are hard for their enemies to see.

The uakari (wah-KAH-ree) is a monkey. Like most monkeys, the uakari is covered with hair. But its face is red and has almost no hair on it. When a uakari gets excited or upset, its face gets even brighter red.

WATCH OUT!

People sometimes use colors to give a warning. Signs that are bright orange or red tell us to be careful. Animals use warning colors, too!

The gila (HEE-la) monster isn't really a monster. It's a lizard. Gila monsters live in the deserts of Mexico and the United States. Their bite is poisonous. The gila monster's orange and black markings serve as a warning to stay away.

There are many kinds of poison dart frogs in South America. They have very colorful markings. The bright colors warn other animals that the frogs are poisonous. Native people apply the poison that comes from the skin of these frogs to darts and arrowheads for hunting small animals.

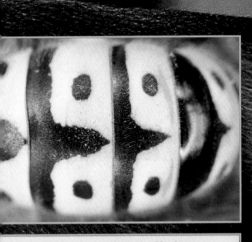

Like this hornet, flying insects that sting are often yellow and black. Think of the bumblebee. Some harmless insects are also yellow and black. By looking like the insects that sting, they are protected from predators.

Mandrills are a kind of baboon. They live in groups. Scientists who have watched mandrills think that the male's bright colors help to tell other mandrills that he is in charge.

BLENDING IN

Some animals have coloring that helps them to blend in with their surroundings. This is called camouflage (CAM-o-flahj) coloring. Green and brown are the most common camouflage colors. But other colors can help an animal blend in.

The wavy brown pattern on this Gaboon viper looks like the dry leaves i is crawling through. This snake some- times hunts by hiding in leaves Then, you might detect its eyes. And that's only if you look very carefully.

This tiny lima shrimp may be bright red, but it is camouflaged. It's the same color as the tentacles of the flame scallop sitting behind it. The shrimp can hide here while it waits for food to come floating by.

See the yellow starfish? It's not camouflaged at all. But do you see the fish beneath it? If this scorpionfish closed its eye, the fish would be almost impossible to see. The scorpionfish hides on the seafloor waiting for prey to swim by.

Spiders that live on flowers sometimes match the color of the petals. You may not even notice that they are there. The spiders hide from insects they hunt, and from animals that would eat them.

PRESTO CHANGE-O!

Color in our skin comes from pigment. Some animals change color by changing pigments in their skin or hair. Certain animals can change color whenever they want. Others change automatically when it's the right time.

The chameleon (kuh-MEAL-ee-un) is a lizard. It changes color quickly to send messages to other chameleons, or to blend in with the background. It also changes color as its mood changes. A frightened or mad chameleon may turn almost completely black.

The octopus can turn many different colors. You can see the colors changing as you watch. The octopus has special, colored parts of its skin that it can make bigger or smaller within moments to hide itself on the seafloor.

Some animals change colors when the seasons change. They are white in Winter to blend with snow, and brown in Summer to mix with the forest floor. This weasel is partway through its seasonal change. It may take several weeks to change all the way.

13

GROWING UP

Our hair gets grayer as we get older. But our skin stays almost the same color our whole life. Many baby animals are colored very differently than their grown-up relatives. Sometimes it is hard to tell they are the same kind of animal.

You would never guess that these are both emperor angelfish. The young fish has circles and spots. The adult has completely different markings and a cool black mask.

baby Brazilian tapir is striped
d spotted like a watermelon!
it gets older, the light marks
ill slowly go away. Then it will
plain brown all over, just like
its mom
and dad.

ese
ds are
h bald
gles. The young,
wn bird won't
its yellow beak,
ite head, and white
feathers until it is four
ive years old. That's
en it will be grown-up.

We are generally the same color all over. Some animals are like this, too. But other animals are covered in stripes, spots, and strange and colorful patterns.

A tiger's orange fur has bold black stripes. The tiger is easy to see in the open. But when tigers are hunting, their stripes help ther to hide. The stripes look like the patterns made by shadow of trees and long grass.

Why does this clown shrimp have big purple spots? This could confuse an animal that's looking for food. The shrimp may not match the predator's idea of a meal. Markings that make an animal's shape hard to detect are called disruptive (dis-RUP-tiv) coloring.

The bright stripes of this racer snake actually help it to hide. The light and dark lines break up the snake's shape, making it hard to see the snake slithering through grass.

t's not certain why giraffes
e spotted. When giraffes are feeding in a grove of trees, their spots
ay make them harder for lions to see. Their markings blend in with
e spots of light that filter through leaves. On the plains, giraffes are
sy to see. But *they* can see long distances, too. They can see
edators coming, and run away.

BOYS AND GIRLS

In people, boys and girls have the same kind of coloring. But in some species of animals, males and females look very different.

If you have pet guppies, you may be wondering why some are more colorful than others. With some kinds of guppies, you can tell the boys and girls apart by their tails. Boy guppies have fancy markings and colors on their tail. The girls are less colorful.

Male frigatebirds have a bright red pouch on their throat. They puff their pouch with air and make noises when they are trying to attract a female. Once a male has a mate, the red color of his pouch starts to fade.

Female peacocks are called peahens. They are mostly gray and brown. But male peacocks have spectacular colors hidden in their big tail. The male opens his tail like a fan to get a female's attention.

If you're a relative of the monkey known as a black lemur, it's easy to tell if you're a girl or a boy. Just look at your fur! If it's jet black, you're a boy. Black lemurs with brown fur are girls.

BRILLIANT BIRDS

Compared to birds, people aren't very colorful. There is a good reason. Birds have the best eyes of any animal when it comes to seeing colors. Birds often rely on color to attract a mate.

Parrots are some of the world's most colorful birds. Many are green, blue, and yellow. This scarlet macaw also has bright, glowing red feathers. Imagine seeing these birds flying over their Amazon rain forest home!

Most birds have brightly colored feathers. But the toucan (TOO-can) can have a rainbow of colors on its beak. Different kinds of toucans have different-colored beaks.

The blue of this malachite (MAL-uh-kite) kingfisher doesn't come from a colored pigment in its feathers. The color is made by light passing through the feathers. This is the same kind of color you see on a soap bubble or an oily water puddle.

Quetzals (ket-SULS) live in Central American rain forests. Their brilliant green feathers were prized and traded by the ancient Maya (MY-uh) people. A quetzal's green tail may grow to 30 inches long!

IN BLACK AND WHITE

Many animals are brightly colored. But there are also animals that are plain black or white. Some are both black and white.

Sometimes this animal is called a black panther. It is really a black leopard. You can see its spots. Instead of yellow with black spots, it is all black because its fur is colored by the pigment melanin (MELL-uh-nin). Melanin is the same pigment that gives our skin its unique color.

The beluga is a white whale that lives in northern oceans. Baby belugas are pale pink when they are born. They gradually turn brown, then dark bluish gray. This color slowly gets lighter. The beluga is finally white when it is about seven years old.

Zebras are easy to recognize, with their black and white stripes. Scientists aren't sure why they have such bold markings. The stripes may break up the zebra's outline and make it harder for predators to see. Or they may help zebras to recognize each other.

This gray squirrel is completely white because it's an albino (al-BY-no). Albinos don't have any melanin to darken their skin and fur. Albinos also have pink eyes because they don't have any pigment to hide the blood that runs through them.

23

BORROWED COLORS

Some animals get their colors in a strange way. The colors don't appear naturally. Often, they come from outside sources such as plants and food.

Sloths are slow-moving animals. They hang from trees in South American rain forests. Their long fur sometimes looks green, but it didn't grow that way. The color comes from tiny plants called algae (AL-jee). The plants live on the sloth's fur.

Wild flamingoes are bright pink. The color comes from pigments in the algae and plankton the flamingoes eat. These are the same pigments that give carrots and tomatoes their color. Flamingoes in zoos sometimes lose their color. But if they are given the right kind of food, they will turn pink again.

The part of this giant clam sticking out between the top and bottom shell is called a mantle. It is very brightly colored. But don't be fooled! The clam's color comes from tiny blue and green algae living in the mantle. 25

UNDER THE SEA

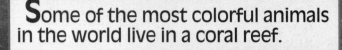

Some of the most colorful animals in the world live in a coral reef.

A reef is made by millions of very small animals called coral polyps (POL-ips). These brightly colored corals provide background for animals that live near the reef. See the red fish swimming around the red coral?

Anemones (uh-NEM-oh-nees) are animals that look like plants. The parts that look like petals are really stinging tentacles. A fish swimming too close will get stung. Then the tentacles pull the fish into the anemone's stomach.

The most extraordinary colors on the reef might belong to the nudibranch (NUDE-uh-brank). Nudibranchs are like snails without shells. They move through water by fluttering the edges of their body.

Many animals are plain old brown and gray. Often, we think these colors are dull. One of the main reasons so many animals are brown or gray is so they can blend in with the background. If you are not noticed, you won't be eaten!

This bat is nocturnal (nok-TURN-ull). It is active at night. Bright colors wouldn't be very useful in the dark. During the day, bats roost in dark or shady places. Plain brown fur helps them to hide and keep safe while they sleep.

Brown feathers help to protect the female mallard. In Spring, she hatches her eggs and spends lots of time sitting on the nest. Her brown feathers blend in with the ground and make it difficult for a predator to see her. Many female birds have brown feathers for this reason.

The pale gray of the shark blends with the color of the ocean. Many fish are gray, silver, or blue for this reason. The color of a shark's skin makes it hard for prey to see the shark approaching.

ephants
e big!
ey don't
ed to be a
ight color to
noticed. And cam-
flage spots won't really
lp them to hide. Plain gray works
ry well for the elephant.